Mortal Beings

Faye Alexandra Rose

Mortal Beings

Copyright © 2022 Faye Alexandra Rose
DARK THIRTY POETRY PUBLISHING
ISBN: 978-1-7397975-5-3

Faye Alexandra Rose
First edition

Artwork by Dewang Gupta via Unsplash

DTPP3

DARK THIRTY POETRY PUBLISHING

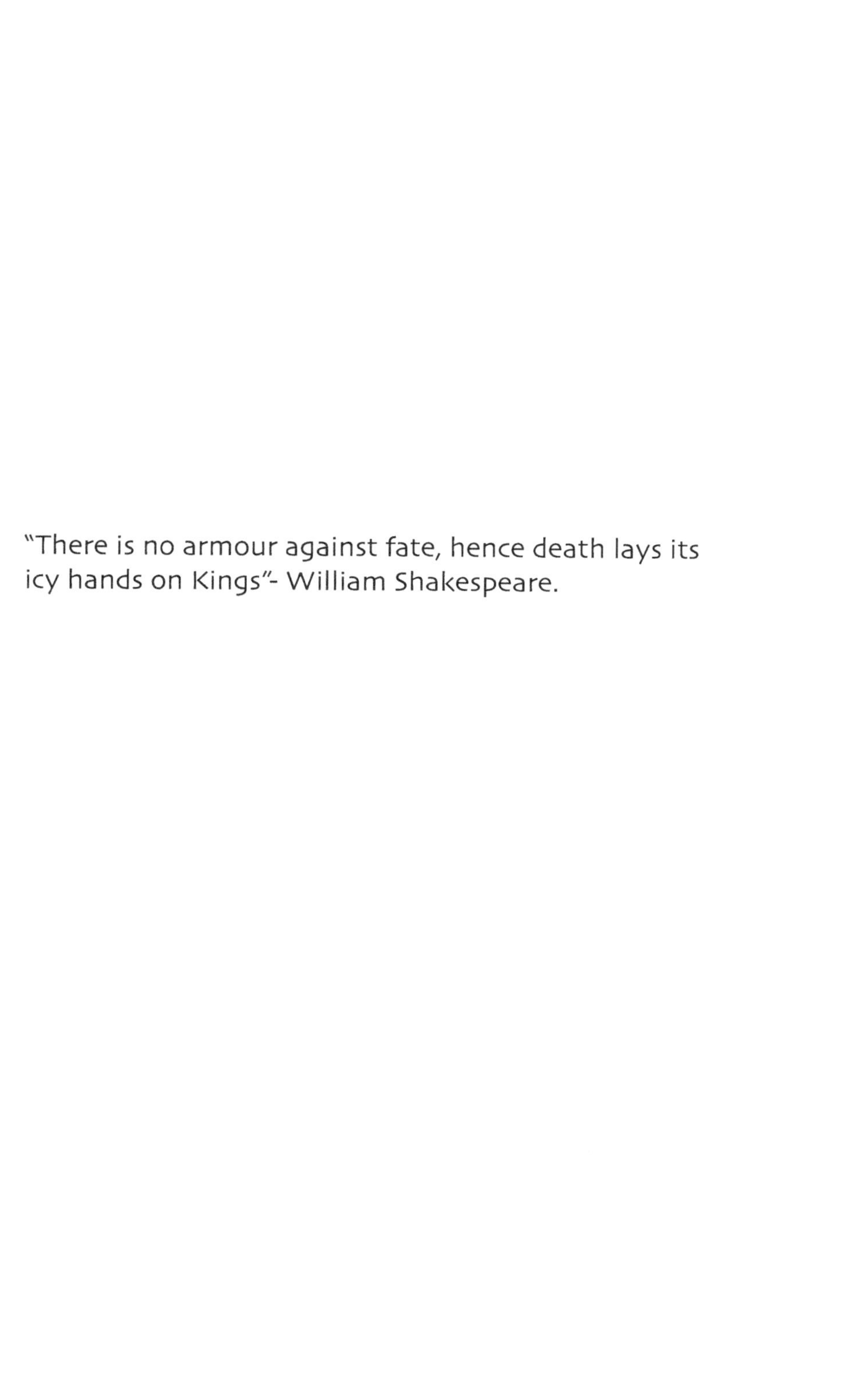

"There is no armour against fate, hence death lays its icy hands on Kings"- William Shakespeare.

Foreword

This collection was written during the second year of my undergraduate degree as part of the module, 'Writer as Researcher'. Originally it consisted of only seven poems, but I extended it to fifteen after graduating.

It explores grief and mourning through different perspectives, allowing the unique practices from various cultures to highlight that death does not need to be final. Writing this collection was extremely cathartic and helped me to process my own loss by understanding death in a way that contrasts with our western ideologies.

The poems are purposefully simple in their forms to allow the unique beauty of each culture to shine through. I wanted to write in a way where I did not speak for them, so I also included references to sources to allow further reading if desired.

Faye Alexandra Rose
January 2022.

Contents

Fantasy Coffins:

"They build fantasy coffins - Okadi Adekai in the local Ga dialect – to represent the deceased's profession, vices or dreams"

We made a chilli pepper in your name,

the colour red does not mean bloodshed

no, it represents your heart

and the fire you had for life.

They will come in their masses

to stand in awe and feast on your stories,

we will celebrate from sunrise to sunset

for you brother,

and radiate from your aura.

A Journey for The Body:

"In the Toraja region of Sulawesi, in Indonesia, the dead are a constant part of day-to-day life."

His bed faces west

to the heavens,

waiting for buffaloes

to sacrifice to the gods;

he is only to macula

so, care for him I must.

He has taken his last breath,

but his soul has not yet transcended

he is himself as much as before,

his life has not yet ended.

Sky Burial:

"In Tibetan Buddhism, sky burial is believed to
represent their wishes to go to heaven."

When the vultures come

we will celebrate.

That a body can keep on giving

even after its final breath.

Day of The Dead:

"El Día de los Muertos, is a Mexican holiday where families welcome back the souls of their deceased relatives for a brief reunion that includes food, drink and celebration."

I see skulls of colour

the vibrancy of death come to life,

as we make our offerings

to the loved ones lost

we celebrate, and

dance in their name.

The spirits take our hands

and we follow their lead

for death is not to be mourned,

life is to be embraced.

Turning of the Bones:

"In a sacred death ritual, ancestors are exhumed every
five to seven years. It's an opportunity to visit a loved
one's corpse, pay respects, and dance with the dead."

Spray him with wine

he must smell like the life he lived,

lay him in my arms

and I'll rewrap him in silk.

Write his name upon the fabric

to not be forgotten,

a feast roasts in his name;

the aroma of home surrounds him

I'll lift his body above the living

in celebration –

Watch us dance with him,

As the warmth fades over the horizon,

we return to the tomb

lay Ariary upon his chest;

a gift towards his second life

because until bones turn to dust,

and his spirit departs us

I will honour him.

*Originally published in Mookychick Magazine, 2019.

Sacred Duty:

"Balinese believe that the human body is only a
temporary shell, which is impure and has no
significance at all."

A dragon,

carved out of our finest Banyan

home grown in your beloved land,

sits patiently beside the bull that houses

your body, to witness the smoke envelop

your soul towards the new vessel.

The Parade:

"A tradition from Varanasi, India involves parading
the dead through the streets, the bodies dressed in
colours that highlight the virtues of the deceased."

Wrapped in red linen,

I watch as our city

raises him towards the sky,

reach salvation.

Bathed in sacred waters,

before erupting into flames

reach salvation,

reach salvation.

Burial Beads:

"Families don't always opt for ashes. Several
companies there compress remains into gem-like
beads… These "death beads" are then displayed in the
home."

Yellow beads lay upon his sister's mantle

tiny spheres,

a galaxy of stars

where he shines the brightest.

Our house has become a home

again,

now that he is back

within its walls.

The Urhobo:

"While most Christians do not believe in witchcraft, the Urhobo do. They also believe there are good deaths and bad deaths. There are requirements for both."

Bad Death

The forest howls

calling for their bodies,

the young taste sweeter,

their souls forever trapped

between teeth.

Good Death

A long life is celebrated

frail body lays peaceful

legs towards the door.

When the canon fires,

wipe your tears,

for its time

to celebrate their spirit.

Stilts:

"The Igorot Tribe have their own unique tradition which dates back thousands of years. A popular tourist attraction, coffins are placed on stilts high up cliffs in the belief that the higher up the body is resting, then the easier their passage to heaven will be."

Pass the final nail

and hammer it into the rock face,

let her body be at one with the clouds,

she is safe now that heaven can see her.

The Smoking Dead:

"The Tinguian people dress bodies in their finest clothes, rest them in chairs and place lit cigarettes in their mouths. The bodies remain in these positions for several weeks."

There is a familiarity to her final moments,

beloved jewels hang around her neck

as she sits, cigarette glowing between her lips.

Her final form, now sat upright within the soil

hands tied to her feet, her ghost cannot roam

now that earth has set her free.

Straight to Heaven:

"The Ganges is the most sacred river to the Hindu faith and is even worshipped as the goddess Ganga. In a concept called 'Moksha', they believe that if the ashes of the deceased are scattered in a holy place (Varanasi being the most holy), they will escape the cycle of rebirth and go straight to heaven."

Watch them drift towards salvation

and bathe in her purity –

rid them of damnation

and allow them security.

Dazzling Death:

"When someone dies, their surviving loved ones often choose to cremate the body. Years ago, most families opted to store the remains inside an urn or sprinkle them somewhere of significance outside. Today, people are choosing a more adventurous option — they're turning ashes into diamonds."

Ashes from molten

now pressurised carbon,

solidifying everlasting

beauty.

Western Celebration:

"A funeral is a ceremony connected with the final disposition of a corpse, such as a burial or cremation, with the attendant observances."

The air feels heavy,

thick with melancholy

as my stomach churns from

the mix of hymns and rain,

crusted tears layer cheeks with

the taste of salted memories, as

her body is lowered within the soil

the lilies wilt with sorrow beside her name

now eternal in stone.

About the Author

Faye Alexandra Rose is a poet and copywriter and the author of Incognito (Bottlecap Press, '22) and Pneuma (Sunday Mornings at the River, '21) which has been shortlisted for a Saboteur Award for Best Poetry Pamphlet. She graduated with first-class honours in Creative and Professional Writing and English Literature and is currently studying for an MA in Creative Writing.

RELEASED BY DARK THIRTY POETRY

ANTHOLOGY ONE
THIS ISN'T WHY WE'RE HERE
MORTAL BEINGS